A Book To Help Teenagers
Cope with the Problems of Loneliness

Other works by Shirley Schwarzrock

Contemporary Concerns of Youth
Effective Dental Assisting
Effective Medical Assisting

Other books in the *Coping with* Series, Revised

Coping with Personal Identity
Learning to Make Better Decisions
Grades, What's So Important about Them, Anyway?
My Life—What Shall I Do with It?
Do I Know the "Me" Others See?

Coping with Human Relationships
Can You Talk with Someone Else?
Appreciating People—Their Likenesses and Differences
To Like and Be Liked
Fitting In
You Always Communicate Something

Coping with Facts and Fantasies
Facts and Fantasies about Drugs
Facts and Fantasies about Alcohol
Facts and Fantasies about Smoking
Food as a Crutch
Facts and Fantasies about the Roles of Men and Women

Coping with Teenage Problems
Crises Youth Face Today
Coping with Cliques
Parents Can Be a Problem
Some Common Crutches
Coping with Emotional Pain

Living with Loneliness

Shirley Schwarzrock, Ph.D.
C. Gilbert Wrenn, Consultant

AGS
American Guidance Service
Circle Pines, Minnesota 55014-1796

Cover Design
Gene Roeckers
Leighton Fossum

Illustrations
Fred Dingler
Sylvia Carsen

© 1984 AGS® American Guidance Service, Inc. All rights reserved, including translation. No part of this publication may be reproduced or transmitted in any form or by any means without permission in writing from the publisher.

Printed in the United States of America.
Earlier edition © 1970 by American Guidance Service, Inc.
Library of Congress Catalog Number: 83-072922
ISBN 0-88671-009-X

THE

SERIES REVISED

Living with Loneliness

discusses

- the difference between being alone and being lonely
- the times when all of us are lonely
- some ways to avoid being lonely all the time
- methods of maintaining a balance between pleasant experiences alone and pleasant experiences with others.

Other books in the *Coping with* Series, Revised, are listed on the back cover.

Contents

That Shut-Out Feeling 1
Loneliness Is Everywhere 3
Situations Creating Loneliness 9
Growth Through Loneliness 17
Everyone Experiences Loneliness 21
Ways of Overcoming Loneliness 23
The Balance 28

That Shut-Out Feeling

Are you ever lonely? Most of us are occasionally — teenagers included. Adults, however, may not recognize when a teen is lonely. Some have forgotten how hard it is to be a teenager. Many adults are so involved in being parents of teenagers that they don't see the world as their kids see it — a world that is often unfriendly.

What *is* loneliness? Why are all people lonely? The dictionary says that *lonely* is "being cut off from others" and implies "longing for companionship"; that *being lonesome* is "to feel sad or dejected as a result of lack of companionship or separation from others." On the other hand, *solitary* implies "absence of others without necessarily having it bother one."

These definitions help us understand. We can be *alone* — without others — and feel all right about it, even be happy being alone. It's when we feel *cut off* that we are lonely. Under what circumstances might you feel cut off?

When you

- can't do as you planned?

- have a dream that is impossible to achieve?
- are separated from a loved one?
- are secretly ashamed?
- experience the death of a loved one?
- are left out of a group to which you want to belong?
- are ridiculed by others and, thus, shut out?
- feel so different you can't belong comfortably?
- have to work while your friends play?
- can't buy the things your friends buy — the clothes, tapes, cars?
- don't dare confide in others because they laugh or tell other people, or are unsympathetic?
- have to stay in and write a paper — and everyone else is going off for fun?
- feel parents are shutting you out, or you assume they are?
- have a tough decision to make — alone?
- find circumstances, such as a divorce or a move to a new neighborhood, have changed your life?
- are in a new environment without much chance to do anything but cope with it?
- realize you have made a terrible mistake?

- are shut out because you don't like the TV program everyone is watching? (You feel bored and lonely with nothing to do.)
- are alone because you don't want to do what everyone else is doing?

These are some of the happenings that make people feel lonely. Actually, anything that makes one feel *cut off* or *shut out* often causes loneliness.

Loneliness Is Everywhere

If you feel lonely much of the time, it might surprise you to learn that others are lonely too — even people who seem to have many friends.

Terry is the most popular girl in school. She has three girlfriends. The foursome is always giggling and doing things together from playing tennis or riding bikes to sitting in the backyard sunbathing. There are four guys who go with these girls. They always go to everything together. Terry is never alone — or so it seems. But sometimes in the middle of a party, Terry will find herself momentarily with nothing to say or do. When this happens, Terry feels strange, and suddenly begins to talk rapidly, with forced excitement, to those around her.

Perhaps she doesn't recognize her feelings of aloneness at this point, but she is suddenly lost in the middle of the crowd. She talks more rapidly and forces herself to be more enthusiastic. She hopes this "hyper" activity will take away the loneliness.

Loneliness can affect anyone. People feel lonely at different times and for different reasons. Some of our most popular leaders are very lonely people. Think of the president of the United States. It is said that is the loneliest job in the land because the president must finally make and stand behind decisions that affect millions of people.

People react differently to being lonely. Some step quietly back into a corner. Others, like Terry, try to become more active and noisy, thinking this is the answer to avoiding loneliness.

Terry may not be aware of her loneliness, but she feels it just as keenly as Mary who is usually alone at school, and who speaks shyly to just a few of her classmates. Mary doesn't often go to parties. When she is pushed into going by her mother, she usually just sits and watches. Everyone knows she is lonely. Most people don't realize Terry is lonely sometimes, too. And what about those teenagers who aren't as popular as Terry nor as alone as Mary? All experience some kind of "shut out" feeling sometimes — some more often than others.

Feeling left out is an unhappy experience. We can't all be popular all of the time, but we can do something to avoid feeling lonely most of the time. It is important to remember that sometimes a popular person *works hard* to *stay* popular even though being popular is only partly satisfying. This may be Terry's problem. She may be afraid to be alone, afraid to try to think for herself. Perhaps she has been taught that a girl *must* be popular. Somehow the message has been given that the girl who is popular in high school has a better future. So Terry must keep herself busy being the most popular girl socially. She has no time to think about what she really wants from life, no time to stop and get acquainted with any one individual more deeply than the others. She surrounds herself with three girls who also try to be popular, but she can't share with anyone her innermost thoughts and hopes. It would be difficult for her to confide in these three girls who are, in a way, competing for the same goal she is — a better future.

Unless Terry can develop a special kind of relationship with a sister, brother, parent, or someone who has no contact with her school life, she actually is very much alone. Her popularity, which to others may seem the greatest of gifts, is only partially satisfying. There are times when she needs more personal relationships with one or two very special people who will help her discover and understand what she really wants from life.

Mary doesn't know how to say the kinds of things other kids want to hear. She is too inhibited to ask questions. Someone has taught her that she is prying if she asks other kids about themselves. She needs to be able to be friendly with others. And being friendly means that you express an interest in the other person's life and affairs. It is true that there are some questions that might be considered prying, but to ask about someone's special project, or what play rehearsal was like, is a good way to show interest. People feel good if they are asked about their special interests: the bike race or computer project they are working on — or anything else that shows real interest in what is important to them.

Sometimes lonely persons are not willing to make the necessary effort to try to be friends with another person. Sometimes they are so uncertain of their own value as persons that they can't think of anything to say. They believe they always mess up any attempts they make to be friendly so they don't try.

Situations Creating Loneliness

Here are some of the situations in which people feel lonely.

1. A person has personal, private dreams that can't be communicated to anyone.

    Tommy feels very inadequate in real life. He is not a good athlete, he is just an average student, and he doesn't seem to do anything outstanding. Tommy dreams of being the president of a large firm, sitting at a huge desk in an extravagant office at the top of the Empire State Building, pushing buttons and having people respond quickly.

    Tommy can't share this dream with anyone! He shuts himself off while he dreams. His classmates leave him alone because they feel shut out. Soon the circle is complete. He avoids the gang to dream certain hours away, and they fail to include him in their activities. He is very lonely.

2. A person has so many friends that she or he can't be close with anyone.

    Remember Terry? She needed someone to be close to her, but she was so busy being popular she didn't have time for closeness with one person. She was lonely in a crowd.

3. A person is afraid to tell anyone his or her fantasies or thoughts for fear of losing a friend.

    Ann has secret sex dreams. She is very much

ashamed of them and is afraid that she will lose the friendships she has at school if anyone finds out about her dreams. She avoids close friendships for fear she might inadvertently say something that would let someone know about her thoughts. She is very lonely with her fear.

4. A teenager feels that she does not have love and support at home. She feels alone in the world. It can happen for several reasons.

Martha's parents both work. In fact, Martha's dad is working two jobs so he doesn't get home until bedtime. Her mother struggles to do the housework evenings, excusing Martha from helping so she can study. On Sundays both parents are so tired that they can hardly talk. Martha knows better than to ask her mother to come to the school concert. She has been told her parents are too tired. Martha understands what her parents have to do — but occasionally feels shut out. Martha is very lonely trying to run her school life without "bothering" her parents about anything.

It doesn't have to be a home where both parents work for teenagers to feel lonely, either.

Doug's parents are always busy, engrossed in their adult activities. Doug's mother is usually away when he comes home from school. She is so busy with her friends and civic activities that she gives Doug little attention. His dad is an executive who works about eighty hours a week. When he does have free time, there are cocktail parties and club events to attend.

Doug rarely sees his parents except at mealtime. When Doug was in the class play, his parents were

pleased, but they didn't attend the play because there was an office party that night. Doug feels that no one in his family really cares about him as a person. He is very lonely.

5. A teenager lacks support at school and feels left out and alone because he is a nonentity there.

Hank is a very quiet boy who doesn't seem to know how to mix well. He rarely raises his hand in class. His teachers don't single him out for praise or approval. Neither do they single him out for disapproval. Hank always turns in his assignments on time, but they aren't anything unusual. He is a C student. Because he is quiet without any outstanding abilities, he is lost in the crowd. Although Hank participates in some extracurricular activities, he is never a leader — always a quiet member. He belongs to Math Club, but sits through the meetings making no contribution. He just doesn't have anything to say.

Hank is lonely.

6. A teenager is very creative but also very lonely.

Jon was taking a required course in art. He suddenly "saw" an old man sitting on the ground and began to fashion him in clay. Soon his teacher was looking on with interest. Then Jon discovered some problems in molding the arms just right and realized he must stay after school and work extra hours if he was to succeed. Suddenly making the sculpture was more important than the game he could play with his friends that afternoon. Jon came to the art room after

school and continued to work alone. Eventually he had created the old man just the way he wanted him. The clay was colored and fired in the kiln. The finished project was placed in the display case outside the art room.

Jon had achieved something during the hours spent alone. It hadn't bothered him to be alone while he sculpted. He rejoined his group the next day, but heard murmurs about how "different" the statue was. A giggle here and there. Suddenly Jon felt lonely, shut out: a result that sometimes comes from creating something original.

Jon feels he can't talk with anyone about his feelings of loneliness. He has realized that he felt great when he was working alone but that he felt lonely and left out when he was with people. Jon has experienced the isolation that many adults accept as part of creating something regardless of what that something is, from creating a mathematical formula to a picture or a character in a play. Creating something is a good feeling to have part of the time, but needs to be balanced with good feeling when others are around.

Creative people frequently experience loneliness. People working alone have contributed great ideas and accomplishments. Great inventors and writers must seclude themselves to accomplish their goals. Einstein needed solitude to evolve the Theory of Relativity. J. D. Salinger chose to retire to a windowless building to write books like *The Catcher in the Rye.*

7. A teenager ends a close relationship and feels cut off and lonely. Perhaps the hardest kind of loneliness to handle is that which comes when you deliberately cut yourself off from someone with whom you have had a close relationship. For example,

Jack and Sue have been going steady. It is a "convenient" relationship: never a worry about whom to take or whether one will have a date. However, Jack and Sue are not really happy together, and Sue finally develops enough courage to break up. Both Jack and Sue will be lonely until they find new friends. It takes courage to force oneself to break off a convenient relationship before one has developed other relationships.

8. A person feels that "No one understands me." This is a common complaint from teenagers and from many adults, too.

Bob enjoyed working with motors. He could think of nothing more enjoyable than to spend his life tinkering with motors. He wanted to be a mechanic. As soon as school was over, he rushed home to work on whatever motor he had been able to acquire. Somehow he just couldn't remember his assignments, nor anything else that wasn't connected with motors.

His parents became very upset with his grades, and his father firmly said, "No more motors. No more time on anything but your school work until your grades are improved."

Bob was frustrated. He tried to explain, but his father was unsympathetic. Bob said, plaintively, "But you just don't understand."

He felt very much alone.

Growth Through Loneliness

Loneliness can help an individual to grow, to become a better person.

All through high school Hal had ignored his "little" sister, Laurie, who was a grade behind him. He was frustrated sometimes because his mother kept nagging him to take Laurie along, or find a date for her. It made him angry because he thought she ought to find her own friends.

Laurie was somewhat shy and had many responsibilities at home because her mother worked and Laurie had to prepare dinner, grocery shop, and do most of the housework. She didn't have the free time and the contacts Hal had. She was very lonely.

Hal never seemed lonely. He had his gang of boyfriends, and there was always something going on: either they were doing something together or they were going to a party with their dates.

When it was Hal's turn to have the gang at his house, Laurie fixed the refreshments but she was never included in the group. They all had their girlfriends.

Laurie felt her loneliness keenly. She looked forward to Hal's parties because it gave her a chance to mingle a little. As time passed, however, she found activities to fill the times of loneliness.

After his graduation, Hal's job on a construction crew took him to a remote part of the country where he saw no one his own age for several months. All his social life and camaraderie disappeared. When he returned to his barracks after a full day of hard work, there was nothing to do and no one he could appreciate. His only outlet was to write letters back home.

A year passed. Hal was able to come home for Laurie's graduation. She was thrilled to have him come.

As they finished eating dinner, Hal stood, picked up dishes and started for the kitchen. Laurie was surprised and followed him, also carrying dishes.

"Mom, you just sit and rest. Laurie and I will clean up the kitchen, won't we, Laurie?" Hal said.

Laurie was surprised and pleased that Hal was helping her do the work that she had always done alone. As they worked, Hal said, "Laurie, I understand how it is now. I'm not going to do anything for fun unless I can fix up a date for you, too. I just didn't know how it was for you — so lonely. And I'm going to do my share of the work here, too."

*Laurie smiled. "Well, Hal, it **was** awful last year, but this year I learned how to enjoy some of the times I'm*

alone. Don't miss a good time on my account. You don't have much time before you have to go back to your job. And it's wonderful to have you helping with the cleanup!"

Hal looked serious. "Well, you'd better teach me how to manage loneliness. I think it's terrible. And I was thoughtless last year."

"Thanks, Hal, for telling me. And if you get a date, we can have some fun. I've been dating Mark Atkinson. He's already suggested that we double date while you're here."

"That's great! I never thought Mark would get around to dating. He's a great guy."

Laurie smiled. "Maybe he's learned the value of being alone like I did last year — and we can both give you some pointers on enjoying some times alone."

Hal had, through loneliness, become more aware of the needs of others. He became concerned about what happened to someone besides Hal, and that was growth. Loneliness can make us grow.

Laurie and Mark had found growth through loneliness in another way. They had found satisfaction in doing some things alone. They also learned about being contented when they weren't at the center of a group. They may have more enjoyable lives because they know how to balance times alone and times with others.

Everyone Experiences Loneliness

When we think of loneliness, we have to accept the idea that loneliness is a very real part of life for most people. An author who writes books for adults tells how lonely he felt, how filled with pain, when he had to decide whether to give permission for his daughter's heart surgery. He mentions how alone they both felt even when they were in the same room as she slowly recovered.

Another person experienced complete loneliness when she was in a foreign city, halfway around the world, and unable to understand the language or be understood. She missed her family. "Shut out" was the only term to describe her feeling. That's the way a teenager can feel — or the teenager's parents — when the walls go up and there is no communication. Sometimes teenagers think they don't dare tell their parents how they feel about having come in second — or not placed — or been first in the race — or that they are "in love" with someone.

Meanwhile the parents are sitting there wanting very much to hear just how the teenager feels. Perhaps they are remembering the way *they* felt to be third in an athletic contest instead of first, or the excitement they felt on their first dates. And so the parents sit there feeling shut out and lonely, and son or daughter also sits there

feeling shut out. They just can't confide their feelings to each other. Everyone is lonely.

Ways of Overcoming Loneliness

So what do we DO about it?

Here are some ideas that have helped other people overcome loneliness. See if they can help you.

Recognize that other people are lonely too, that sometimes it's *our* attitude that shuts others out and makes them — or us — feel lonely. Try to refrain from shutting others out for at least a part of the time each day. Concentrate on showing an interest in *their* lives and interests. Each time we concentrate on someone else, we make it easier to do. Gradually we overcome the habit of shutting others out.

Look around for someone who is lonely or ill at ease — less comfortable than you. Make a real effort to do something with this person. Take the initiative. Concentrate on one person at a time, and be interested in getting that person to do something with you. If you never ask anyone to do something with you, you will be alone more than is necessary. Doing

something for another makes you feel needed and therefore less alone. It may be simply singling Hank out to say, "Hi, how are things going?" Gradually you will come to know Hank. It really isn't hard to do, but it is necessary to find someone who needs to have friends. This isn't likely to be the most popular person in your class. It may be someone as shy as you or even less comfortable than you. Perhaps it is someone who doesn't seem particularly outstanding — just one of your classmates who goes to school every day, like Hank. Asking Hank to do something with you (like go to a game) may make him feel needed — and you will begin to find the companionship you need.

Another idea is to plan something for a Friday or Saturday night. Ask someone or several kids to come to your house if you can't afford to go to a show. Popping corn, making candy, watching TV, or listening to records can be fun. And really be *with* your guest or guests. Concentrate on listening. Remember that listening and responding to what you hear will make all of you feel better. You will get to know each other and all will feel less lonely.

Trust someone, and you may discover you have made a close friend. Of course, when we trust another we are taking a risk, one that many of us are afraid to take because we fear that the person we trust may betray our trust. On the other hand, we may discover that our trust is not betrayed — and then we can trust in comfort

— and will feel less lonely. *Anything* worthwhile involves some risk, but doing nothing is riskiest of all.

Join a group where members share their dreams and fears. Counseling groups are often formed in schools. In these groups, group members realize that all of us have fears and dreams and that all experience similar emotions. No one is really alone.

Some people say they find it hard to make that first effort to join a group. It is difficult; but if you do take that first step and go to a meeting, you usually find it easier to continue going and you find some members you like. Friendships usually follow. People who want to overcome loneliness will force themselves to change their environment. One good way is to join a group.

Plan some times to be alone. Plan to do something you can enjoy alone. It's important to learn to be contented when you're alone because there are times when each of us is alone. What are activities that can be done alone? Any creative craft work, reading, and shop or home-making activities help make time spent alone pass quickly. The person who becomes interested in building a boat or designing a dress usually becomes so absorbed in the project that the time alone passes quickly. Being alone can be an opportunity to create something very worthwhile, and that kind of aloneness must be experienced by anyone who wants to do something individual.

The Balance

Life has to be a balance of companionship with others and companionship with oneself. Each of us has the ability to choose activities with others and activities we like to do alone. So if you are lonely, you can do something about it!

You can:

- recognize that other people are lonely, too, and avoid shutting others out,
- look for someone who is lonely and try to be friendly,
- trust someone,
- join a group who share their fears and dreams,
- plan some time to be alone, and learn to enjoy your own company.

Accept the times of aloneness and balance them out with time spent with others. Remember that being alone can be a rewarding part of life if you can just keep from being terrified at the prospect. It can help you be creative. You can understand how others feel about being alone and be more compassionate. And you can learn to be a better companion and develop friendships with others who also have times when they feel alone.

Teenagers wonder a lot . . . feel a lot . . . worry a lot. But too often, they don't say a lot.

CONTEMPORARY CONCERNS OF YOUTH

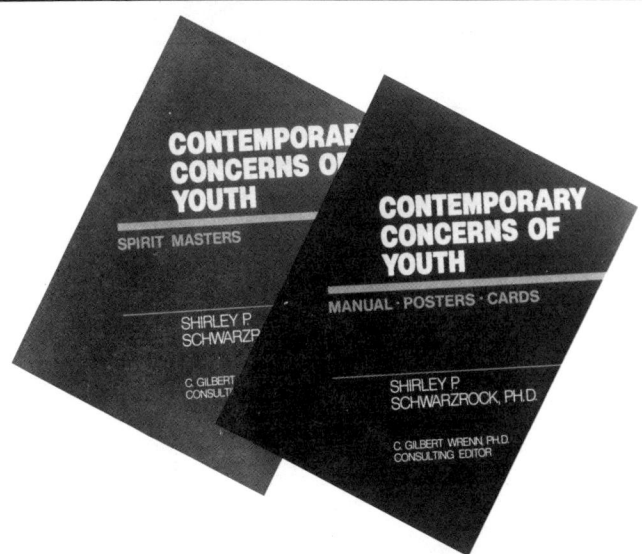

Timely materials that encourage young people to express themselves on the issues that most concern them.

Contemporary Concerns of Youth reaches out with discussion topics, lively activities, and recommended readings that focus on young people's needs. The 36 units fall into these four categories:

Know Thyself

Relationship to Others

Survival Skills

School-Related Concerns

Materials include:

Leaders' Manual: 36 units for discussion; including background information, instructions for student activities, recommended readings.

85 Duplicating Masters: stories, ideas, questionnaires, and exercises.

Posters and Communication Cards illustrate key ideas, promote discussion.

Available from

AGS®

Publishers' Building
Circle Pines, MN 55014-1796.

THE BOOKFINDER

A GUIDE TO
CHILDREN'S LITERATURE
ABOUT THE NEEDS AND PROBLEMS
OF YOUTH AGED 2-15

The right book at the right time can help you find solutions . . . gain insights . . . understand that you are not alone.

Let's say you've got a problem. And you really don't know which way to turn. Picking up a book can help a lot. But what book? The Bookfinder will help you find books so that you can:
- work through your own dilemmas by seeing how other people have solved similar problems
- gain insights into your personality and values
- recognize your abilities and self-worth
- enjoy reading and become a better reader.

How it works:
First go to a library and ask for The Bookfinder. Using the subject index, look through the more than 450 topics:

belonging	boy-girl relationships
courage	death
divorce	embarrassment
fighting	friendship
homosexuality	jealousy
parents	pregnancy
prejudice	rape
sex	siblings
weight control	

For each topic, as many as a dozen books may be listed. Read the synopses to help pick the book that's right for you. Finally, check out and read the complete book!

Ask your librarian for The Bookfinder today!

The Bookfinder is a three-volume reference available from AGS. For more information write or call Publishers' Building, Circle Pines, MN 55014-1796.   612-786-4343.